MW00712095

contents

in recent times I've had the opportunity to experience, first hand, children involved with the Make-A-Wish Foundation. It has made me realise how insignificant our day-to-day problems are compared to those with a life threatening illness. These children have been the stimulus for putting this book together and calling upon my business connections in the hope that we can make a difference. It has been wonderful for me to see the meat industry unite in support of such a worthy cause and help some of these special children to achieve their dreams.

flying home

when asked what she would wish for most in the world, one little wish recipient responded that she would like to "go home and have a picnic". Home was the Kimberley in the far north of WA and the five-year-old had not been there for some time due to the need to be in Kununurra Hospital for her treatment.

in conjunction with a helicopter company, The Make-A-Wish Foundation arranged for her to fly home with her mother and nurse for a day. The Kimberley community travelled down to Glen Hill in a convoy of 4 wheel drives and a bus to attend the picnic, which had been organised on the school oval. Their presence, along with the clowns (which had been particularly requested), helped create the magic for this very special little girl.

it is stories like this that have made me passionate about doing everything I can to improve the quality of life for these most deserving children.

the contents of this book have been inspired by the roasts and casseroles and soups that warmed my stomach as a child growing up in the back blocks of Melbourne and the aromas and flavours that transformed these dishes from just simple meals to fond memories. Some have a contemporary twist, and all have a story to tell.

i don't believe in just eating to live but rather I believe in living to eat. And why not? After all, we spend nearly twenty percent of our waking hours indulging ourselves in the noble arts of preparing and consuming food.

i am not a chef, but a retailer, in particular a meat retailer. That's why the focus of this book is not just on creating gourmet delights to tempt and tantalise the foodies amongst us, but a genuine effort to explain some of the finer points of meat, what you should look for when you buy it, how to prepare it and the myriad ways you can cook it.

our lifestyle has changed dramatically over the last three decades. Multiculturalism, longer working hours and more women in the work place have all contributed to altering the way we buy, store and prepare food. Health experts tell us we should eat meat, trimmed of fat and in more moderate amounts. However, for most of us, meat does continue to grace the centre of the dinner plate and, I'm delighted to say, looks like doing so for a long time to come.

the supplier of that meat, the butcher shop as we know it, is closing at a great rate and may not be so lucky. Gone is the old wooden chopping block, the sawdust on the floor and the bloodstained apron. The word of the butcher was unquestioned, someone you could trust. There was always time for a chat and some friendly advice on the best cut of meat for the job. You didn't have to ask, you would be told whether you wanted to know or not.

quality assurance programs spelt the demise of the sawdust and chopping block, we started to find those bloodstained aprons unpalatable to look at and our new busy lifestyles didn't leave us much time for a chat. Our lifestyle changed but the meat industry and its product didn't. The way we purchased meat became less convenient. Supermarkets seized the opportunity and started to tray pack meat and moved the butchers into the backroom.

with the introduction of improved quality systems and a new meat grading system for beef (Meat Standards Australia) that guarantees tenderness or your money back, once again we are seeking out specialised meat stores that can give us the quality of meat we are looking for. The product is leaner and trimmer and so are many of the butchers. A new look meat store is starting to open its doors. So perhaps the butcher shop may have a life after all.

there is an old saying that nothing really changes it just re-invents itself and this is never truer than when talking about food. Whether it's butcher shops or the product they sell. Lamb shanks, osso bucco, even beef cheeks and lamb's liver are regaining popularity at the hands of some of the country's most prominent chefs.

in retrospect, how fortunate was I? These were all everyday meat products in my mother's kitchen when I was growing up.

several of the recipes inside come from my mother, some I've adapted to more modern flavours and all have fond memories. While you're salivating over the chicken and lemongrass soup or the Moroccan lamb, take time out to have a look in the hints section. There is a wealth of basic information about meat, what to look for when you buy it and which cuts are best to use for which dishes. I've tried to keep it simple, and hopefully, it will answer some of those questions about meat that you've always wanted to know, but were afraid to ask.

barely a day goes past that we don't enjoy the many taste sensations of beef in one way or another. Unlike the juicy big steaks of twenty years ago, people today appreciate the unique qualities of beef transformed into kebabs and hamburgers, wrapped in pastry or breadcrumbs or served with sauces and marinades gathered from all over the world.

these days we all want the process of food shopping and preparation made easier, and when it comes to beef, we also want tenderness and flavour.

it's easy to talk about selecting perfect beef, but how do you go about it and where do you find it? With the introduction of it's Meat Standards Australia program, Meat and Livestock Australia is making sure the beef we purchase has a high degree of quality and tenderness. The new standards program will also help you work out which beef cuts are best used for different cooking purposes. Make sure your butcher is part of the Meat Standards program, and ask their advice about what best suits your needs.

for convenience today, you can buy smaller portions, trimmed of fat, tender and succulent – and there is a lot more to be done with a good piece of beef than just tossing it on a barbecue. Many cuts are great for casseroles, stir-fry or roasts. Washed down with a good bottle of red, they create some of my favourite meals.

in this section, you will find how different cuts of beef can be transformed into mouthwatering dishes for any occasion. Take a trip around the world or just down memory lane with these simple, full of flavour recipes.

beef

beef rib
chilli soup

1 tablespoon olive oil
4 **beef spare ribs**, halved
Rib Rub
1 tablespoon cracked black pepper
1 tablespoon sea salt
1 teaspoon cumin powder
Soup Base
1 tablespoon olive oil
2 medium onions, finely chopped
3 cloves garlic, crushed
½ cup of tomato paste
1 teaspoon dried basil
1 teaspoon dried oregano
1 teaspoon hot chilli powder
1 litre tomato juice
1 x 810g tin chopped tomatoes
1 cup beef stock
1 x 420g tin kidney beans, drained
1 x 420g tin soybeans, drained

1 recipe jalepeno cornbread,
    see page 70

Heat oil in a sauté pan and brown ribs to seal.
Remove from pan and place in baking tray.
Mix rub ingredients together and rub over ribs.
Bake in a 180°C oven for 1½ hours or until ribs
are tender.

Meanwhile sauté onion and garlic in oil until
translucent. Add tomato paste, dry herbs and
chilli powder. Cook for 3 minutes before
adding tomato juice, tomatoes, stock and
beans. Bring to the boil, then reduce to simmer
for 1 hour.

Remove ribs from pan and leave to cool,
reserving pan juices. Shred meat, discarding
bones and fat. Add meat to soup, heat through
and serve. For a richer soup, chill meat
drippings and remove fat. Simmer liquid to
reduce and add to soup.

corned beef hash

Serves 4

1 tablespoon olive oil
1 tablespoon butter
2 cloves garlic, crushed
1 onion, finely chopped
300g cooked **corned beef** in
    1cm cubes
4-6 medium potatoes, cooked
    and cut into 1cm cubes
1 tablespoon dijon mustard
3 tablespoons chives,
    chopped
black pepper to taste
4 poached eggs

1 recipe caper hollandaise
    sauce, see page 67

In a large sauté pan, heat oil and
butter, add garlic and onion and
cook until translucent. Add the
corned beef, followed then by the
potatoes and heat through. Stir in
the mustard, chives and pepper.
Serve topped with one poached
egg per person and drizzle with
caper hollandaise.

*If you have some leftovers from
your corned beef dinner, try this –
it's so simple and full of flavour*

mediterranean sausages with chickpea and artichoke mash

Serves 5-6

Sausage Mix
800g beef mince
1 tablespoon tomato paste
1 egg lightly beaten
1 tablespoon fresh thyme
    leaves
100g black pitted olives,
    chopped
100g pimento stuffed green
    olives, chopped
¼ cup fresh basil, roughly
    chopped
2 or 3 small red chillies,
    de-seeded and finely
    chopped
4 spring onions, finely
    chopped

3 tablespoons olive oil

Sauce
350g tomato pasta sauce
½ cup tomato paste
¼ cup fresh basil, roughly
    chopped

1 recipe chickpea and
    artichoke mash,
    see page 66

Combine sausage mix ingredients.
Divide mixture into 10 equal
portions. Moisten hands with
water and roll each portion into a
sausage shape. Seal sausages by
frying in 2 tablespoons olive oil.
Combine sauce ingredients. Pour
remaining tablespoon of oil into
the bottom of a small roasting
pan. Place sausages in pan and
cover with combined sauce ingredients. Bake uncovered in a 180°C
oven for 35 minutes. Serve with
chickpea and artichoke mash.

sirloin steak with wasabi and ginger butter

Serves 4

4 x 200g **sirloin steaks**
Wasabi Butter
200g butter, softened
1 teaspoon wasabi powder or
    2 teaspoons wasabi paste
1 teaspoon fresh ginger,
    peeled and grated

In a hot pan or BBQ, cook the sirloin to medium rare. Set aside to rest.

Add the wasabi and ginger to the butter and mix well. Serve the steaks topped with the wasabi butter.

beef and white bean tortillas

Serves 4

500g **blade steak**, sliced
Marinade
1 teaspoon onion flakes
2 cloves garlic, sliced thinly
1 teaspoon ground coriander
1 teaspoon ground cumin
½ cup vegetable oil
White Bean Mash
2 x 400g tins cannellini
    beans, drained
¼ cup sour cream
¼ cup spring onions,
    chopped
pinch of chilli flakes
salt to taste

6-8 corn tortillas
1 tablespoon olive oil
100g lettuce leaves

1 recipe avocado and
    capsicum salsa,
    see page 66

Combine marinade ingredients and add sliced steak. Marinate for at least 2 hours in refrigerator. Meanwhile, pulse bean mash ingredients into a paste in a food processor. Grill meat, set aside and keep warm.

To assemble, heat olive oil in a large pan and quickly brown both sides of all tortillas. Place tortillas on a serving dish, divide mash evenly and spread. Top with lettuce leaves and warm beef slices. Finish with avocado and capsicum salsa.

layered loaf

Serves 4-6

Mince Mix
500g **beef mince**, lean
½ medium onion, finely chopped
½ cup crispbread, finely crushed
2 tablespoons dijon mustard
3 tablespoons tomato paste
2 cloves garlic, crushed
1 egg, lightly beaten
2 tablespoons oregano, finely chopped
1 tablespoon sea salt
1 tablespoon cracked black pepper

100g baby spinach, blanched and
    drained well
1 large roasted red capsicum,
    see page 68
Glaze
2 tablespoons tomato paste
2 tablespoons seeded mustard

In a large bowl, add mince mix ingredients and mix well. Lightly grease a non-stick loaf tin. Place ⅓ of the mince mix in an even layer on the bottom of the loaf tin, follow with a layer of spinach, ⅓ of the mince mix, the roast capsicum and finish with a ⅓ layer of mince mix. Smooth surface, cover with foil and bake in a 180°C oven for 30 minutes.

Remove from oven, combine glaze ingredients and spread evenly over the surface. Return uncovered to the oven for a further 15 minutes. Before serving, rest in the tin for 5 minutes.

Using a spatula, gently slide loaf out of tin onto a cutting board and slice. Serve hot or cold.

Every butcher has their own interpretation of beef mince (choice, premium, supreme etc), but 100% lean beef mince gives the best result.

beef niçoise with seeded mustard dressing

Salad
2 x 200g **rib eye steaks**
100g black olives
1 medium red onion, sliced thinly
250g green beans, blanched
4-6 chat potatoes, cooked and quartered
4 roma tomatoes, chopped
4 hard-boiled eggs, sliced
400g mixed lettuce leaves
Dressing
2 tablespoons seeded mustard
1 cup olive oil
½ cup balsamic vinegar
zest of 1 orange
1 teaspoon white sugar
1 clove garlic, bruised
salt and black pepper to taste

Whisk dressing ingredients and set aside. Char grill steaks to medium rare and allow to rest while you prepare the salad. On a large platter (or individual plates) scatter the lettuce leaves and top with the remaining salad ingredients. Slice the steak and arrange over the salad. Drizzle dressing over the salad and serve.

For special occasions it's worth the little extra for eye fillet, but for everyday use you can also use blade or round steak cut thinly.

grilled beef medallions with prawn cream

*8 x 100g **beef eye fillet medallions***
Sauce
1 tablespoon butter
1 tablespoon olive oil
2 cloves garlic, crushed
250g green prawns, peeled and finely chopped
½ cup cream
1 tablespoon fresh parsley, finely chopped

Heat the butter and oil in a sauté pan. Add garlic and prawns, and sauté until prawns are cooked through. Add cream, and reduce to thicken. Take off heat and add parsley. Set aside and keep warm.

Grill medallion steaks to medium rare. Place 2 medallions on each plate and top with prawn cream sauce.

Eye fillet is the ideal cut for this recipe, but rib or scotch fillet makes a good alternative for the budget conscious.

prime rib roast with seeded mustard glaze

*2½kg **rib roast** on bone, trimmed*
Glaze
2 tablespoons seeded mustard
2 tablespoons creamed horseradish
2 tablespoons brown sugar
1 teaspoon fresh rosemary, finely chopped
1 teaspoon freshly cracked pepper
½ teaspoon sea salt flakes

Score the surface of the roast with a checkerboard pattern. Combine the glaze ingredients and spread over the meat surface.

Place in a roasting dish and bake in a 180°C oven for 2 hours or until meat is medium rare. Rest for 15 minutes. Slice to serve.

Ask for the rib roast with chine bone removed, for easy carving. If this is not available from your local butcher, a boneless cut such as rib fillet, scotch fillet or cube roll is just as good.

sirloin wrapped asparagus with a caper aioli

Serves 4

*2 x 150g **sirloin steaks***
2 large bunches medium sized asparagus

1 recipe caper aioli, see page 66

Grill steaks to medium rare, set aside and keep warm. Trim the asparagus to a 6cm tip (reserve the stalks for other uses), blanch and refresh. Slice the steaks on an angle against the grain, making long thin strips.

To assemble, bundle 3 asparagus tips and wrap bases with 2 strips of beef. Drizzle each wrap with caper aioli. Serve with extra caper aioli on the side.

asian beef broth with green tea noodles

Serves 4

1 litre beef stock
1 tablespoon olive oil
*250g **topside steak***
200g green tea noodles
5cm fresh ginger, peeled and cut into fine matchsticks
1 clove garlic, finely chopped
2 spring onions, finely chopped
200g asian mushrooms, chopped
1 tablespoon soy sauce

1 recipe infused lemon oil, see page 67

Pour the stock into a large pan and gradually bring to the boil. Meanwhile, heat oil in sauté pan and cook the steaks until medium rare. Set aside and keep warm. When the stock is boiling add the noodles, ginger and garlic and reduce heat to simmer for 5 minutes. Add spring onions and mushrooms and allow to simmer for a further 3-4 minutes or until the noodles are tender and the mushrooms heated. Slice beef thinly. Pour broth into bowls, and top with warm beef slices. Drizzle with the lemon oil and serve immediately.

wonton ravioli

Serves 4-6

Filling
250g _rib eye steak_
1 tablespoon oil
1 tablespoon tomato paste
1 cup red wine
1 cup beef stock
1 teaspoon white sugar
2 garlic cloves, bruised
½ medium red onion, sliced
1 stalk rosemary
Caramelised onions
1 tablespoon butter
2 medium onions, sliced
1 tablespoon brown sugar

1 pack wonton wrappers

For filling, heat oil in sauté pan, add garlic, onions and rosemary and cook until onions are translucent. Add beef to seal then remove from pan. Add tomato paste to pan and stir for 1 minute. Add wine, stock and sugar and heat through. Return steak to pan, cover and simmer for 5 minutes. Remove steak from sauce. Strain sauce, keep warm and put to one side.

To caramelise onions, heat butter in a clean sauté pan, add onions and cook until translucent. Sprinkle with sugar and cook on low heat until onions have caramelised.

To assemble, thinly slice steak. Lay one wonton wrapper down. Place 1 teaspoon of onions and 1 slice of steak in middle, paint edges with a little cold water and top with second wrapper. Seal edges.

Bring a large pot of water to a slow simmer and add wanton ravioli in small batches, cooking until wonton wrappers are tender.

Drain wonton ravioli, place on plate and drizzle with heated, strained sauce and serve.

As the beef is sliced thinly, most quality cuts of beef will work in this recipe.

marinated brisket rolls

Serves 4-6

500g **beef brisket** point end, lean
Marinade
1 teaspoon black pepper
½ medium onion, sliced
2 garlic cloves, bruised
4 stems thyme
½ cup dry white wine
½ cup olive oil
Spread
½ cup fresh herbs, finely chopped
   (chives, parsley and thyme)
1 small clove garlic, finely chopped
250g spreadable cream cheese
1 tablespoon sour cream
salt and black pepper to taste
Filling
5 pieces wholemeal mountain bread
   (or any other middle eastern flat bread)
50g alfalfa sprouts
1 carrot, peeled and grated
½ small red onion, finely sliced
½ red capsicum, fine julienne

Combine marinade ingredients and pour over brisket in a small, deep sided roasting tin. Cover with foil, and bake in a 180°C oven for 1½ hours.

Mix spread ingredients to create a smooth paste.

When brisket is cooked, remove from pan and slice thinly, then return to pan with cooking juices and allow to cool.

To assemble, lay out a piece of bread. Spread cheese mix over entire surface. At the short side, lay a handful of the vegetables the entire length, then top with slices of brisket. Roll into cylinder, and cut in half on an angle.

marinated beef with fresh asian noodles

Serves 4

500g **beef topside steak**,
   thinly sliced
Marinade
1 tablespoon mirin
   (rice wine vinegar)
2 tablespoons black bean
   sauce
2 tablespoons soy sauce
juice of 1 lime

2 tablespoons peanut oil
2 cloves garlic, finely
   chopped
4 spring onions, sliced on an
   angle
2 cups beef stock
350g fresh udon noodles
1½ cups snowpeas, julienne
1 medium carrot, julienne
1 red capsicum, julienne
1 tablespoon cornflour,
   dissolved in 2 tablespoons
   of cold water

1 recipe chilli dressing,
   see page 67

Combine marinade ingredients and add sliced beef. Marinate for 1 to 2 hours in refrigerator. Heat peanut oil in a very hot wok and add garlic, spring onions and meat. Cook until meat is sealed, remove from wok and set aside.

Add vegetables to wok and stir-fry until tender. Add stock and noodles, bring to the boil and add cornflour. Stir continuously until sauce has thickened. Add meat and heat through.

Serve immediately, drizzled with chilli dressing and topped with chopped peanuts, coriander and extra chillies if desired.

citrus scented carpaccio

Serves 6

400g **beef eye fillet**
Dressing
½ cup olive oil
juice of ½ lemon and
   ½ orange
cracked black pepper to taste

zest of 2 lemons and
   1 orange
fresh basil leaves for garnish

Place eye fillet in freezer for approximately 2 hours or until beef is firm but not frozen through. Slice beef wafer thin and place on individual serving plates.

Combine oil with juices and pepper. Drizzle over carpaccio and scatter zest and basil leaves to garnish. Serve with extra dressing on side.

Don't be tempted to use anything other than beef fillet and premium olive oil for this recipe. As this is served raw, ensure that the freshest fillet is purchased.

they used to say Australia was carried on the sheep's back. I've always preferred a nice lamb leg myself and there's no better meat than fresh, small, spring lamb seasoned with traditional garlic and rosemary or mint. Grab this product when available.

these days, of course, lamb can be enjoyed at any time of year, and, when complimented with the myriad of flavours found around the world, it can be transformed into a gourmet's delight. Today we embrace the multi cultural flavours of the Mediterranean and tuck into moussaka or souvlaki with the same fervour that we attack the more traditional Northern European styles. Irish Stew, Shepherd's Pie and Lamb Shanks have all come back into vogue and why not? They are simple and sensational.

when looking for true lamb, always look for a red brand stamped on the piece of meat. No brand will usually denote the meat as mutton, which is older and much stronger in flavour. This isn't necessarily a negative if cooked in strong flavoured dishes like curry, but again, discuss your individual needs with your local butcher and let them help point you in the right direction.

in this section, you'll find simple ideas aplenty to make your next lamb meal something different and very special.

lamb

chunky tomato and shank soup

Serves 4-6

Shank Braise

4 **lamb shanks**
1 tablespoon oil
3 cloves garlic, crushed
1 large onion, quartered
2 cups red wine
2 cups beef stock or water
2 tablespoons tomato paste
2 tablespoons black peppercorns

Soup

1 tablespoon olive oil
2 cloves garlic, crushed
1 large onion, diced
2 bay leaves
3 medium carrots, diced
3 stalks celery, sliced
3 tablespoons tomato paste
¾ cup brandy
1 litre tomato juice
1 x 810g tin whole tomatoes, chopped
2 tablespoons brown sugar

¼ cup cream
¼ cup fresh basil, chopped

Heat oil in sauté pan, add lamb shanks, garlic and onion. Brown meat and transfer sautéed ingredients to a roasting pan. Add remaining braise ingredients and cover pan with foil. Bake in a 180°C oven for 2 hours or until tender. Remove shanks and discard braise ingredients. Remove meat from shanks when cooled.

For soup, heat oil in a large saucepan and add next 5 ingredients. Sauté until onion is translucent, then add tomato paste, cook for a further 2 to 3 minutes. Add brandy and reduce. Add in tomato juice, tomatoes, brown sugar and shank meat, leave to simmer for ½ hour over low heat.

Remove from heat, add cream and basil and serve immediately.

26

lambs fry with roasted capsicum pesto

Serves 4

400g **lamb's liver**, sinew
  removed and sliced
8 rashers bacon, rindless
2 small eggplants, thickly
  sliced
4 red capsicums, roasted and
  quartered, see page 68
100g mixed lettuce leaves
2 tablespoons olive oil

1 recipe capsicum pesto,
  see page 69

Heat grill and brush with a small
amount of oil. Brush eggplant
with remaining oil, and grill with
liver and bacon.

To assemble, divide all ingredients
into 4 equal portions and stack
alternating ingredients. Serve with
Capsicum Pesto.

*Ask your butcher to cut the liver
thinly. Soak in cold water and
remove the skin to ensure the
liver will not be tough.*

forequarter chops with barley and vegetables

Serves 4

2 tablespoons olive oil
2 cloves garlic, crushed
1 large onion, sliced
4 **forequarter lamb chops**,
  halved
2 medium carrots, sliced
½ cup dry white wine
1 cup pearl barley
4 cups beef or vegetable
  stock
½ cup curly fresh parsley,
  chopped
2 tablespoons fresh thyme
  leaves
100g snow peas, cut in half
100g baby spinach leaves

In a heavy saucepan heat oil and
add garlic, onions, chops and
carrot. Cook until onions are
translucent and meat has browned.
Add white wine and reduce
slightly. Add barley, stock and
herbs, cover pan and bring to the
boil. Reduce heat and simmer for
45 to 60 minutes, or until barley is
tender. Add snow peas and
spinach to heat through. Serve
immediately.

*Use chump chops for a full
flavoured substitute if you wish,
but make sure they are well
trimmed of fat.*

grilled lamb on turkish bread

Serves 4

400g **lamb scotch fillet**, sliced thinly
Marinade
½ cup ouzo
¼ cup lemon juice
1 cup olive oil
1 tablespoon honey
½ cup fresh mint, roughly chopped
2 cloves garlic, sliced
1 teaspoon black pepper

100g lettuce leaves
100g black olives, pitted
½ red onion, finely sliced
2-3 roma tomatoes, chopped
1 x 300g loaf turkish bread

1 recipe minted yoghurt drizzle,
  see page 68

Combine marinade ingredients and lamb. Marinate in refrigerator for 5 hours or overnight, stirring occasionally. Hollow out middle of bread so that it resembles a pizza crust. Grill meat. To assemble, place lettuce in bread, arrange grilled meat then spoon over minted yoghurt drizzle. Top with olives, red onion and tomato. Cut into slices and serve.

The sweetest lamb comes from the forequarter, but you can use any lamb cut in this recipe.

sake lamb

Serves 4

2 x 200g _lamb steaks_
Marinade
1 cup sake
½ cup soy sauce
2 cloves garlic, bruised
2cm fresh ginger, peeled and
grated
1 tablespoon sesame oil
1 cup peanut oil

½ cup soy sauce
½ cup japanese pickles
¼ cup wasabi paste

Combine marinade ingredients and add lamb steaks. Stir well, and marinate for at least 1 hour in the refrigerator, stirring occasionally. Grill steaks for 3-5 minutes on both sides. Serve rare with side dishes of soy sauce, japanese pickles and wasabi paste.

Have butcher cut these from leg, and pound out steaks to 3cm thickness.

parmesan and herb crusted lamb loin

Serves 4

2 _lamb loins/backstraps_,
cut in half
Crust
100g parmesan cheese,
grated
½ cup mixed fresh herbs,
chopped (rosemary, chives
and parsley)
1 cup breadcrumbs
2 cloves garlic, crushed
black pepper to taste

1 recipe parsnip mash,
see page 68

Place crust ingredients in a processor and pulse to form a dry paste. Pour mix on a plate and roll lamb through, coating thoroughly. Place lamb in a lightly greased baking tray. Sprinkle remaining crust mix on top and cover with foil. Bake in a 180°C oven for 15 minutes. Remove foil, then bake for a further 10 minutes or until crumbs are browned. Serve with parsnip mash.

Whilst spring lamb is always great, the loins of slightly larger lambs are better value for money. Lamb rump is also suitable.

savoury lamb filo parcels

Makes 24

2 tablespoons olive oil
2 cloves garlic, crushed
1 medium onion, finely chopped
500g **lamb mince**, lean
1 tablespoon fresh oregano, finely
   chopped
3 tablespoons tomato paste
zest of 1 small lemon
2 tablespoons lemon juice

2 tablespoons butter, melted
16 sheets filo pastry (12 x 26cm)
poppy seeds and/or sesame seeds

Heat oil in a large sauté pan and cook garlic and onions until translucent. Add lamb and cook through. Add oregano, tomato paste, lemon zest and juice. Simmer for 3-4 minutes, then remove from heat and allow to cool.

Take 2 sheets of filo (covering the remaining with a damp cloth to prevent drying out), and brush with melted butter between the sheets. Divide into 3 equal strips roughly measuring 12 x 8cm. Place 1-2 tablespoons of filling along short side of strip, roll half way and turn edges in to contain filling. Continue to roll into a cigar shape, and brush end of strip with butter to seal. Brush butter over parcels and sprinkle with seeds.

Bake parcels on a greased tray at 200°C for 10-15 minutes. Serve with your favourite tomato relish.

Ask your butcher to mince best quality lamb for this recipe – you may need to order it in advance.

lamb and coconut bake

Serves 4

500g **lamb shoulder**, cubed
1 tablespoon plain flour
2 tablespoons vegetable oil
2 cloves garlic, sliced
1 large onion, sliced
1 tablespoon garam marsala
1 teaspoon cinnamon
1 teaspoon turmeric
300g pumpkin, peeled and
    cubed
1 x 400ml tin coconut cream
½ cup shaved coconut

Toss lamb in flour. Heat oil in a large sauté pan and add garlic, onion, meat and spices. Sauté until lamb is browned. Take off heat and stir in pumpkin and coconut cream.

Place mixture into a small, deep casserole dish and cover with lid or foil. Bake in a 180°C oven for 45 minutes. Uncover dish and sprinkle with coconut shavings. Cook uncovered for a further 15 minutes until coconut is toasted and meat is tender.

mini lamb roasts with spiced fetta

Serves 4

4 x 200g **lamb backstraps**,
    butterflied
Stuffing
125g fetta cheese, crumbled
1 tablespoon cream cheese,
    softened
¼ teaspoon nutmeg
¼ teaspoon allspice
¼ cup breadcrumbs
100g spinach, blanched,
    drained well and chopped
cracked black pepper to taste

Mix stuffing ingredients together, divide into 4 equal portions. Splay out lamb, lightly flatten and spread stuffing on each. Roll and truss securely.

Lightly grease shiny side of foil, wrap around each roast and put in roasting tray. Bake in a 180°C oven for 25 minutes. Allow to rest for 10 minutes, unwrap, slice and serve.

This seasoning is sensational and could be used in any other lamb roast. Try a small deboned leg.

We love our
Lamb

31

lamb and sweet potato tarts

Serves 4

500g diced, trimmed or cubed **lamb**
2 tablespoons plain flour
Filling
2 tablespoons olive oil
2 cloves garlic, crushed
1 medium onion, sliced
1 tablespoon fresh rosemary leaves,
    chopped
1 teaspoon cinnamon
¼ cup red wine
½ cup vegetable or chicken stock
2 cups sweet potato, diced and cooked
Topping
¼ cup breadcrumbs
2 tablespoons fresh chives, chopped

1 tablespoon butter, melted
1 sheet puff pastry

1 recipe lemon and rosemary
    mayonnaise, see page 72

Toss lamb in flour. Heat oil in a large sauté pan and add garlic and onion. Sauté until onion is translucent, then add meat and brown. Add rosemary, cinnamon and red wine. Reduce the wine mixture, stirring constantly, then add the stock and sweet potato. Keep stirring until sauce has thickened, then remove from heat.

To assemble, cut pastry sheet into 4 equal squares and trim corners to make circles. Place circles on a lightly greased non-stick baking tray. Divide filling between each circle leaving a 1cm edge. Mix topping ingredients together and sprinkle over each tart.

Bake in a 220°C oven for 15 minutes or until pastry is golden brown.

moroccan lamb

Serves 4

*500g **lamb rump**, cubed*
2 tablespoons plain flour
2 tablespoons olive oil
1 large onion, sliced
1 medium fennel bulb, sliced
1 tablespoon fresh ginger, grated
1½ cups vegetable or chicken stock
2 teaspoons turmeric
1 tablespoon lemon juice
juice of 1 orange
100g dried apricots, roughly chopped
100g raisins
1 pear, peeled, cored and diced
100g pinenuts
salt and pepper to taste
zest of 1 orange

Toss lamb in flour. In a deep saucepan heat oil and add onion, fennel and ginger. Sauté until onion is translucent, then add lamb and brown well. Add stock, turmeric and juices. Cover pot and simmer on low heat for 45 minutes. Add apricots, raisins, pear, pinenuts, salt and pepper. Leave pot uncovered and cook for a further 15 minutes. Sprinkle with orange zest and serve with your favourite rice.

Lamb rump is used for texture in this recipe, but most lean cuts will do, cubed or even sliced thinly. This is an exotic dish perfect for special occasions.

with people seeking more variety in what they eat, there is no doubt that the consumption of chicken has increased.

consistency and ease of preparation is what people are looking for today. Combining the versatility of their product with inventive marketing, the poultry industry has taken the humble chicken from a rare appearance at the Christmas dinner table to an everyday product. Meanwhile, it's pretty difficult to imagine what can be done with poultry that Lenard's hasn't already presented. Well, we keep working on new poultry products to suit our changing tastes and continue to stock those that have become popular standards. The process never ends.

while chicken enjoys huge popularity, other varieties of fowl are becoming trendy and more readily available. Spatchcock, duck and quail are not uncommon on today's restaurant menus and there is a lot of interest in turkey for it's low fat content.

in this section, you'll find some of my favourites with a twist, plus a few new concepts. Simple, tasty and quick to prepare – what more could you want?

fowl

grilled chicken quesadillas

Makes 4-6 quesadillas

2 **skinless chicken breasts**, butterflied
Marinade
juice of ½ lime
2 tablespoons fresh coriander, roughly
    chopped
1 clove garlic, roughly chopped
Filling
100g fetta cheese, crumbled
100g aged cheddar, shredded
2 spring onions, chopped
2 teaspoons fresh thyme leaves
2 tablespoons fresh coriander leaves

1-2 tablespoons olive oil
8-12 flour tortillas

Combine marinade ingredients and add chicken.
Marinate whilst making filling. Combine filling
ingredients, mixing gently.

Grill chicken until cooked and slice into strips.

To assemble, take one tortilla and place on it
2 tablespoons of filling, followed by a few
chicken strips, then another 1 tablespoon of
filling, and top with another tortilla.

Heat oil in a pan and place one quesadilla to
cook over low heat. Cover pan and cook for
2 to 3 minutes or until browned. Carefully flip
the quesadilla and brown for a further 2 to 3
minutes. Keep cooked quesadillas warm whilst
you continue to cook the remainder. Serve
immediately.

butterflied soused spatchcock

2 spatchcocks, butterflied
Marinade
1 cup olive oil
½ cup gin
1 tablespoon allspice berries, crushed
3 bay leaves, torn
3 cloves garlic, bruised
4 sprigs of thyme or lemon thyme, crushed
zest of 1 lemon
juice of 1½ lemons
1 tablespoon sugar

Combine marinade ingredients and pour over birds. Marinate in the refrigerator for at least 3 hours, turning birds every 20 minutes. On a hot grill or BBQ sear both sides of the spatchcocks and place skin side up in a lightly greased roasting pan. Baste birds with marinade and bake in a 180°C oven for 45 minutes.

Spatchcock is young chicken, size 4-6. Most Lenard's stores would be able to order them for you. This marinade is great for any cut of poultry.

chicken thighs topped with pistachio pesto

Serves 4

4-6 skinless **chicken thigh** fillets
Pesto
100g pistachio nuts, unsalted
¾ cup olive oil
2 cloves garlic
100g rocket leaves
salt and pepper to taste
zest of 1 lemon

Add pesto ingredients, excluding lemon zest, to a food processor and pulse to a paste. Stir in lemon zest. Top chicken thighs with pesto and bake covered with foil for 20-25 minutes in a 180°C oven.

Thigh meat is more succulent than breast. This recipe works best with the skin and bone removed.

aromatic chicken and lemongrass soup

6 cups chicken stock
3cm knob fresh ginger,
    fine julienne
1 stalk lemongrass, bruised
2 kaffir lime leaves
2 cloves garlic, finely sliced
2 **skinless chicken
    breasts**, finely sliced
2 spring onions, chopped
½ cup fresh coriander,
    chopped
1 fresh red chilli, finely
    chopped
1 teaspoon fish sauce
1 large bunch baby bok choy,
    roughly chopped
juice of 1 lime
1 tablespoon soy sauce
50g snow pea shoots

Add first 5 ingredients to a large saucepan and bring to the boil. Turn heat down to simmer. Add remaining ingredients except snow pea shoots. Return to the boil. Remove from heat and stir in snow pea shoots. Remove lemon grass stalks and serve immediately.

chicken and brie parcels with raspberry chilli jam

Makes 22-24 Parcels

1 tablespoon olive oil
2 rashers rindless bacon,
    finely chopped
300g **chicken mince**
2 tablespoons fresh chives,
    chopped
50g brie in 1cm cubes
1 pack wonton wrappers
1 egg white, slightly beaten
4 cups vegetable oil

1 recipe raspberry chilli jam,
    see page 71

Heat oil in sauté pan and add bacon, chicken mince and chives. Sauté until chicken is cooked through. Allow to cool.

Take 1 wonton wrapper and lightly brush edges with egg white. Place a teaspoon of the chicken mix in middle of wonton and top with 2 or 3 cubes of brie. Pull corners together and pinch seams, sealing the parcels well.

Heat vegetable oil in small saucepan and deep fry in small batches until golden brown. Serve with raspberry chilli jam as a dipping sauce.

Chill brie to keep firm during preparation. Chicken mince is always available at your local Lenard's store

sweet peppers with chicken and roasted vegetable couscous

Serves 4

Stuffing
1 cup couscous
1½ cups chicken stock
1 tablespoon olive oil
*200g **chicken mince***
1 onion, finely chopped
2 cloves garlic, crushed
1 cup roasted vegetables, chopped
1 tablespoon fresh oregano, chopped
1 tablespoon fresh basil, chopped
black pepper to taste

12 sweet banana peppers
2 tablespoons olive oil

Heat stock and pour over couscous. Stir well and set aside.

Heat oil, sauté onion and garlic. Cook until onions are translucent, then add chicken and cook. Combine chicken mix with couscous, roasted vegetables, herbs and black pepper to taste. Slice stalks from peppers and remove seeds. Pack each pepper firmly with 2 to 3 tablespoons of stuffing.

Place peppers on a greased baking tray and drizzle with olive oil. Roast in a 180°C oven for 20 minutes.

Roasted red capsicum, sweet potatoes and zucchini were used for this recipe, but use any of your favourite vegetables.

43

asian glazed duck

Serves 4-6

1 size 21 **duck**
Poaching Liquid
3 star anise
4 cinnamon sticks
1 onion, sliced
2 cloves garlic, bruised
2 tablespoons black peppercorns
2 bay leaves
½ cup soy sauce
4 litres water
Glaze
1 cup spicy plum sauce
¼ cup soy sauce
2 teaspoons ground cinnamon

Wash duck thoroughly, especially inside the cavity. Add poaching ingredients into a large stock pot and bring to the boil. Add duck, topping up with water if necessary to cover the bird. Return to boil and reduce to a simmer. Cover pot, leaving lid ajar, and simmer for 40 to 45 minutes.

Remove duck from pot and place on a rack in a roasting pan. Combine glaze ingredients and brush the duck, reserving half for basting. Bake duck for 45 minutes in a 180°C oven, basting every 20 minutes.

It used to be difficult to find duck out of the festive season, but Steggles now have duck available throughout the year.

44

teriyaki chicken with sesame biscuits

3 **skinless chicken breasts**, sliced
2cm fresh ginger, julienne
1 cup teriyaki sauce
Sesame Biscuits
¾ cup self-raising flour
⅓ cup water
1 teaspoon sesame oil
1 egg white, lightly beaten
1 tablespoon white sesame seed
1 tablespoon black sesame seed
1 tablespoon sea salt

1 recipe vegetable pickles, see page 70

Marinate chicken, ginger and teriyaki together.

Make pickles and biscuits while meat is marinating. To make biscuits, combine flour, water and sesame oil to form a dough. Roll out very thinly and cut into small squares. Brush squares lightly with egg white. Combine seeds and salt and sprinkle on each square. Bake biscuits in a 220°C oven for 7 minutes or until brown.

Take chicken out of marinade mix and grill. Serve with pickled vegetables, biscuits and a bit of teriyaki sauce.

This recipe is also sensational when made with chicken tenderloins.

turkey and asian mushroom pie

Filling
1 tablespoon olive oil
3 cloves garlic, crushed
1 medium leek, sliced
2 spring onions, chopped
300g mixed asian mushrooms ie: shitaki, enoki, shimeji
2 teaspoons fresh sage, finely chopped
2 teaspoons fresh marjoram, finely chopped
500g **skinless turkey breast** or **thigh meat**, cubed
½ cup chicken stock
½ cup sparkling white wine
½ cup cream
1 tablespoon cornflour, dissolved in 2 tablespoons of cold water

1 sheet short crust pastry
1 tablespoon butter, melted
2 teaspoons white sesame seeds

To make filling, heat oil in a large sauté pan and add garlic, leek, spring onions and mushrooms. If shitaki mushrooms are large, slice. Cook until vegetables are soft. Add herbs and turkey and cook until turkey has browned. Add stock, wine and cream, bring to a slow boil. Add cornflour mix, stirring constantly until thickened.

Pour filling into a deep casserole dish. Top with the sheet of pastry, sealing edges well. Cut decorative vents in pastry, brush with melted butter and sprinkle with sesame seeds.

Bake in a 220°C oven for 25-30 minutes, or until pastry is golden brown.

honey and soy glazed chicken drumsticks

Serves 4

12 medium **chicken drumsticks**
1 small bunch sage
Marinade
½ cup honey
½ cup soy sauce
3 tablespoons olive oil
2 cloves garlic, crushed

Combine marinade ingredients.

Push 1 or 2 sage leaves under the skin of each drumstick and cover with marinade. Refrigerate for a minimum of 2 hours or overnight, turning occasionally.

Place chicken on a lightly greased, foil lined baking tray and bake in a 180°C oven for 35-40 minutes.

If you're feeling lazy, try out Lenard's Chinese honey drumsticks – it's an oldie but a goodie!

baked field mushrooms with turkey

Serves 4

4 large field mushrooms
Topping
350g turkey mince
1 medium onion, sliced
2 cloves garlic, crushed
3 tablespoons fresh chives, chopped
1 medium leek, halved, washed and sliced
100g baby spinach, blanched, chopped and drained well
50g butter, melted
¼ cup breadcrumbs
¼ cup parmesan cheese, grated
1 teaspoon cayenne pepper

Combine topping ingredients, mixing well. Trim stems at base of mushrooms and top each with ¼ of turkey mix.

Place mushrooms in non-stick lightly greased roasting pan and cover with lightly greased foil. Bake in a 180°C oven for 25 minutes. Remove foil and bake for further 5 minutes or until golden.

This is also great with button mushrooms and used for finger food or appetisers. If you can't get turkey mince you can use chicken mince as an alternative.

Lenard's
A TASTE FOR EVERYONE.

chicken maryland with dates and prosciutto

Serves 4

4 *chicken marylands*
Stuffing
1 tablespoon olive oil
2 spring onions, chopped
2 cloves garlic, crushed
1 tablespoon fresh tarragon leaves,
   chopped
½ cup dates, roughly chopped
200g cream cheese, softened
4 thin slices of prosciutto, chopped
⅓ cup bread crumbs
cracked black pepper to taste
Rub
2 tablespoons olive oil
2 tablespoons sea salt

Heat oil in sauté pan and add spring onions, garlic and tarragon leaves. Sauté for a few minutes then remove from heat. Add to rest of the stuffing ingredients in a bowl and combine well. Allow to cool.

To stuff the marylands, run your fingers under the skin of the thigh and leg to form a pocket. With a spoon, put ¼ of the stuffing under the skin and smooth to form an even layer. Seal in the mix by securing the skin of the opening to the flesh with wooden skewers. Rub skin with olive oil and sea salt.

Place marylands in greased baking tray and cover with greased foil. Bake in a 180°C oven for 30 minutes. Uncover and bake for a further 15 minutes to crisp skin. Remove skewers prior to serving.

double turkey breast with cherry and jasmine rice stuffing

Serves 4-6

2.5kg **turkey buffe** or **double breast**, bone in
1 cup butter, melted
Rice Stuffing
1 bay leaf
1 teaspoon ground cardamom
1 teaspoon cinnamon
1 medium onion, halved and thinly sliced
1 tablespoon olive oil
1½ cups jasmine rice
3 cups chicken stock
black pepper to taste
¼ cup curly fresh parsley, chopped
½ cup fresh cherries, pitted and quartered
1 slice of any bread

1 recipe old fashioned turkey gravy, see page 70

To make stuffing, place ingredients, except parsley, cherries and bread, in a non-stick saucepan. Bring to the boil, reduce heat so that it is barely simmering. Cover and cook for 15-20 minutes or until rice is tender and liquid is absorbed. Let cool, and mix in cherries and parsley. Stuff neck cavity of turkey breast, covering neck aperture with the slice of bread to retain stuffing.

Place turkey in a large roasting pan and brush with ½ the melted butter. Cover turkey with lightly greased foil and bake in a 180°C oven for 1½ hours. Remove foil, baste with remaining butter and bake uncovered for a further ½ hour. Serve with stuffing and gravy.

chicken liver risotto

Serves 4

1 tablespoon olive oil
3 cloves garlic, crushed
1 medium onion, chopped
1 heaped tablespoon fresh sage, roughly chopped
1 cup brown mushrooms, sliced
2 cups arborio rice
1½-2 litres simmering chicken stock
pepper to taste
parmesan shavings
50g butter
4 large bacon rashers, lean, rindless and diced
400g **chicken livers**, sinews removed

In a large heavy based pot, heat oil, add garlic, onion, sage and mushrooms. Cook until mushrooms are tender, add rice. Sauté for 3-4 min, stirring continuously. Add 2 cups of simmering stock and stir occasionally until absorbed. Continue adding stock in this fashion until rice is tender. Heat butter in a separate sauté pan and add bacon and livers. Sauté 7-10 minutes until livers are just cooked. Add mixture to risotto and stir gently through.

Serve topped with freshly chopped sage and parmesan shavings. Serve immediately

It is becoming more difficult to get livers today because stringent quality control procedures have made it unprofitable for many chicken producers. Most Lenard's stores still carry livers. Over cooking of livers will make them dry and crumbly.

Lenard's
A TASTE FOR EVERYONE.

poached duck breast salad with orange vinaigrette

Serves 4

4 *skinless duck breasts*
Poaching Liquid
peel of 1 orange (no pith)
juice of 1 lemon and 1 orange
2 cloves garlic, bruised
3 cinnamon sticks
10 whole cloves
1½ litres water to cover breasts
Salad
400g mixed lettuce leaves
½ medium red onion, sliced finely
1 orange, peeled and sectioned

1 recipe orange vinaigrette, see page 71

Place poaching ingredients in a large pot. Bring liquid to a boil then turn down to a simmer. Add the duck breasts and cover the pot. Leave to simmer for 20 minutes. Meanwhile, make vinaigrette. Remove duck and place immediately into vinaigrette. Allow to cool.

Arrange lettuce leaves on a platter. Slice or shred duck, then scatter on top of the salad. Scatter onion and orange sections. Pour remaining vinaigrette over salad and serve.

Duck breasts may be hard to get even if ordered in advance – try your local Lenard's store. Chicken breast is not as sweet but makes an acceptable substitute.

Lenard's
A TASTE FOR EVERYONE.

i guess these days most pork is used for smallgoods, which is a bit of a pity because, cooked correctly, it is a very nice meat.

larger pigs, grown for bacon, don't have a lot of natural flavour and tend to be a bit dry unless cooked perfectly. Fortunately, trendy boutique butchers and the availability of smaller, more succulent pork are leading a resurgence of interest in this meat as more than a middle rasher accompaniment for Sunday's eggs. Keep asking your butcher for smaller, younger pork and ultimately you'll get what you're after. Trust me, it is well worth persevering.

commonly used as a base in oriental cuisine, pork can be enjoyed as a spicy, savoury or sweet meat and will often be found taking pride of place in Chinese, Thai, Vietnamese and Korean restaurants alike. Pork chops and apple sauce, while still a family favourite, has given way to small succulent leg roasts, shaslicks and bratwurst sausages.

sharing a similar versatility to poultry, a whole new generation is discovering how pork can extend their range of pleasurable meat experiences. The recipes in this section will enable you to do some great things with pork – so have a crackling good time.

pork

herbed pork bolognese

Serves 4

1 teaspoon olive oil
3 cloves garlic, crushed
1 medium onion, finely chopped
1 tablespoon fresh oregano, finely
  chopped
½ cup fresh basil, roughly chopped
500g **pork mince**
3 tablespoons tomato paste
½ cup red wine
1 x 810g tin chopped tomatoes
1 tablespoon white sugar
1 tablespoon balsamic vinegar
salt and freshly ground pepper

500g thick egg noodles

Heat oil in a large pan and sauté the garlic and onion until translucent. Add the herbs, then the mince and brown. Stir in the tomato paste and cook gently. Add wine and allow to reduce. Add tomatoes and bring to a simmer for 20 minutes. Stir through the sugar, vinegar, salt and pepper to taste.

Serve with egg noodles cooked to instructions on packet.

Make sure you specify lean minced pork from your butcher or Lenard's store for this recipe.

baked ham with spiced blood orange glaze

Serves 6

1kg **Lenard's ham**, rind on
Glaze
⅓ cup orange marmalade
1 tablespoon blood orange
   juice
2 tablespoons brown sugar
¼ teaspoon ground
   cardamom

Score ham with a checkerboard pattern. Combine the glaze ingredients and brush over the ham. Place in a roasting pan and bake in a 180°C oven for 40 minutes.

Lenard's ham is not available all the time, but this recipe is great for the festive season or any time you can get it

ham hock and yellow split pea soup

Serves 4-6

1 tablespoon olive oil
2 medium onions, diced
3 cloves garlic, crushed
1 tablespoon ground cumin
½ tablespoon ground
   cinnamon
2 bay leaves
1 x 700g **ham hock**, skinned
500g yellow split peas
½ cup fresh parsley, chopped
2 litres vegetable or chicken
   stock

1 recipe tarragon vinegar,
   see page 72

Heat oil in a large saucepan, and sauté the onion, garlic, cumin, cinnamon and bay leaves until the onion is translucent. Add the skinned hock, peas, half of the parsley and pour in stock. Bring to the boil and reduce to a simmer for 45 to 60 minutes, or until peas are tender. Remove from heat and take out ham hock. Remove meat from the bone, shred and return to the soup. To serve, scatter with remaining parsley and a drizzle of tarragon vinegar.

pork stuffed baked apples

Stuffing
300g pork mince
2 large shallots, finely chopped
1 clove garlic, crushed
2 tablespoons fresh flat leaf parsley, chopped
1 tablespoon butter
¼ teaspoon ground fennel seeds
½ teaspoon caraway seeds
1 cup savoy cabbage, finely shredded

4 large or 8 small red or green apples
2 tablespoons olive oil

Combine the first 4 stuffing ingredients together. In a sauté pan, heat butter then add remaining stuffing ingredients and sauté until cabbage is tender. Let cool. Add cabbage mix to pork mix and combine well.

To prepare apples, cut around and remove the stalk. Create a pocket using a melon baller (be careful not to gouge the sides or base). Fill the pockets with the stuffing, lightly drizzle with oil and bake uncovered at 180°C for 20 minutes.

Granny Smith apples are perfect for this recipe as their tartness complements the herbs.

pork spare ribs with bourbon and maple glaze

Serves 4

1.5-2kg **pork spare ribs (american style)**, cut into 5 ribs per portion
Poaching Liquid
1 tablespoon black peppercorns
5 cloves garlic, whole
2 bay leaves
water to cover ribs
Glaze
1 cup maple syrup
½ cup bourbon
3 tablespoons tomato paste
2 teaspoons cayenne pepper

Place ribs and poaching ingredients in a large pot. Bring to the boil, then turn down to simmer and cook for 45 minutes.

Combine ingredients for glaze. Remove ribs from poaching liquid and dip into glaze, thoroughly coating each piece.

Place ribs on a foil lined and lightly greased baking tray and bake in a 200°C oven for 10 minutes. Baste with remaining glaze and bake for further 10-15 minutes until glaze has caramelized.

If you prefer a bit more meat on your bone, ask your butcher for pork shoulder chops and get them split through the seam.

vietnamese pork balls

Serves 4

Pork Ball Mix

500g pork mince
2 cloves garlic, roughly chopped
1 tablespoon soy sauce
1 tablespoon fish sauce
1 tablespoon white sugar
2 tablespoons vietnamese mint, roughly
    chopped (Use coriander if
    unavailable)
1 tablespoon cornflour
3 drops of sesame oil

1 cup peanut oil for frying

1 recipe vietnamese dipping sauce,
    see page 72

Combine ingredients in a food processor and pulse until it forms a paste. Moisten hands with water and roll meat mixture into walnut sized balls.

Shallow fry small batches of balls in peanut oil on low heat until cooked through (5-7 minutes), turning occasionally. Serve on wooden skewers with vietnamese dipping sauce.

Make sure you specify lean pork mince from your butcher or Lenard's store for this recipe.

butterflied pork steaks with fennel and prosciutto

Serves 6

6 **boneless pork steaks**, *butterflied*
Filling mix
1 tablespoon olive oil
1 medium onion, halved and thinly sliced
1 clove garlic, crushed
½ cup fennel tops, chopped
1½ cups fennel, thinly sliced
2 tablespoons apple juice
6 thin slices prosciutto

1 cup breadcrumbs
1 tablespoon butter, melted

1 recipe pear and apple relish,
  see page 73

Heat the oil in a pan and gently sauté the onion, garlic, sliced fennel and fennel tops and cook until translucent. Add the apple juice, allow to reduce and remove from heat to cool.

Open the steaks and lay one slice of prosciutto on each steak. Divide fennel mix evenly between steaks and fold over, securing each with a wooden skewer. Place steaks in a lightly greased roasting pan. Cover with foil and bake in a 180°C oven for 20 minutes. Mix the breadcrumbs and butter, remove foil from pan and sprinkle mix over steaks. Return to oven and bake uncovered for a further 5 minutes or until breadcrumbs are browned. Remove skewers before serving. Serve steaks on top of pear and apple relish.

tandoori pork fillets

4 pork fillets
½ cup tandoori paste
½ cup plain yoghurt
1 teaspoon cumin

1 recipe herbed wild and
basmati rice, see page 73

Combine tandoori paste, yoghurt
and cumin. Coat fillets with the
mix and marinate for 1 hour.

Place fillets on a greased baking
tray, and bake at 180°C for 20-25
minutes. Serve with herbed wild
and basmati rice.

*Butterflied pork rib or pork scotch
fillet will also work well in this
recipe.*

cajun pork strips

Serves 4

300g pork fillet strips
Crumbing Mixture
2 cups plain flour
3 tablespoons cajun
seasoning, hot or mild
2 egg whites
1 cup breadcrumbs
3-4 cups vegetable oil for
frying
extra cajun seasoning to
sprinkle

1 recipe capsicum
mayonnaise, see page 72

In a small bowl combine flour and
seasoning. Place breadcrumbs and
egg whites in separate bowls. To
crumb strips, first roll in flour,
then egg white, then breadcrumbs.

Heat oil in a small saucepan and
deep fry strips in small batches.
Drain on paper towel and sprinkle
with more seasoning if desired.
Serve with capsicum mayo.

*Only use pork fillet strips for this
recipe. It also works well with
chicken.*

pork loin roast with nectarine and brioche stuffing

Serves 6

1.5-2kg **boneless pork loin roast**,
  skin scored

Stuffing

1 tablespoon butter
2 cloves garlic, crushed
1 medium onion, finely chopped
2 nectarines, chopped
2 tablespoons fresh sage, chopped
½ cup pinenuts, toasted
4 cups brioche, cubed
½ cup chicken stock
1 egg, lightly beaten
salt and pepper to taste

For Crackling

juice of 1 lemon
¼ cup olive oil
2 tablespoons sea salt flakes

Over a low flame, heat butter in sauté pan and add garlic and onions. Mix and remove from heat. In a bowl, add stuffing ingredients to onion mix and combine well. Splay roast, flesh side up, and spread stuffing to cover. Roll roast, placing seam side down, truss with kitchen string.

Place roast in a roasting pan, seam side down, and rub skin with lemon juice, then oil, then salt. Roast uncovered at 220°C for 45 to 60 minutes or until skin has crackled sufficiently. Lower oven temperature to 180°C and bake for a further 45 to 60 minutes until cooked through.

This seasoning is truly unique, and its flavour is great with any pork roast.

warm pork and prawn glass noodle salad

Serves 4

1 tablespoon oil
4 tablespoons fresh ginger, grated
2 spring onions, chopped
300g green prawns, peeled and deveined
300g **pork fillet strips**
100g each of julienne snow peas, carrot
   and red capsicum
1 tablespoon soy sauce
½ cup thai sweet chilli sauce
100g glass noodles, cooked

2 tablespoons fresh coriander, chopped
300g mixed asian lettuce leaves
1 tablespoon black or white sesame
   seeds

Heat oil in a very hot wok, then add ginger, onions, prawns and pork. Stir-fry to seal the meat. Add vegetables and cook until tender, then add the sauces and noodles. Stir constantly until noodles are heated through. Remove from heat and let cool slightly.

Place coriander and asian greens in a large serving bowl and pour wok mixture on top. Combine quickly, and serve topped with a sprinkle of black or white sesame seeds.

Any cut will do for this recipe, but make sure you ask for retail pork, not small goods.

ever dreamed of a bit on the side? Well, this section has lots of them. Dressings and sauces, mustards and salsa, every meal needs those little extras to lift it above the mundane.

extras add those explosions of flavour that bring the finishing touches to a meal. The possibilities are endless, supermarkets and delis are full of them, and these days, there are even specialty stores that sell nothing else. They're great out of a bottle, but even better when they're made fresh.

in this section you will also find rubs and marinades, chutney and relish, to enhance or garnish. Some of these extras will go with almost any meal, so don't use them only for the specified dishes. Their versatility is only restricted by the bounds of your imagination.

extras

avocado and capsicum salsa

1 tablespoon vegetable or olive oil
¼ teaspoon ground cumin
¼ teaspoon garlic powder
¼ cup fresh coriander, chopped
1 red capsicum, diced
1 avocado, diced
juice of 1 lime
cracked black pepper and sea salt
  to taste

Mix all ingredients together gently and serve.

See recipe page 12.

chickpea and artichoke mash

1 x 400g tin chickpeas, drained and
  mashed
800g marinated artichoke hearts,
  roughly chopped*
½ cup olive oil
2 cloves garlic, crushed
juice of 1 lemon
cracked black pepper and sea salt
  to taste

Mash the chickpeas and artichokes. Heat the oil in sauté pan, add garlic and then the mash. Heat through, stirring continuously. Add the lemon and salt and pepper to taste. Serve hot.

*or 800g grilled, marinated artichokes
  from your deli.

See recipe page 11.

caper aioli

juice of ½ lemon
2 teaspoons dijon mustard
2 egg yolks
3 cloves garlic, finely crushed
1 cup olive oil
1 tablespoon capers, roughly chopped
2 tablespoons fresh parsley, roughly
  chopped (flat or curly)

Combine the lemon juice, mustard, egg yolks and garlic in a processor or blender. Gradually add oil in a fine stream whilst blender is running. Pour sauce into a jug or bowl, and stir capers and parsley through.

See recipe page 16.

caper hollandaise sauce

2 large egg yolks
2 tablespoons lemon juice
200g butter, melted
1 tablespoon capers, roughly chopped
salt and cracked black pepper to taste

Combine egg yolks and lemon juice in a food processor. Add melted butter in a fine stream whilst processing. Pour sauce into a jug or bowl and stir through the capers, adding salt and pepper to taste.

See recipe page 11.

chilli dressing

2 teaspoons white sugar
¼ cup peanut oil
¼ cup light soy sauce
1 whole chilli, de-seeded and finely chopped
1 teaspoon fresh ginger, finely chopped

Add all ingredients, and whisk until well combined.

See recipe page 19.

infused lemon oil

1 cup vegetable or peanut oil
zest of 1 lemon

Gently warm oil. Remove from heat, add lemon zest. Pour into a glass jar and store away from light.

See recipe page 16.

beef stock

2-3kg beef bones, cut into
*   8-10cm pieces**
3 brown onions, quartered with skin on
2 carrots, roughly chopped
2 stalks celery, roughly chopped
¼ cup tomato paste
3 tablespoons olive oil
5 stems fresh parsley (curly or flat)
2 large bay leaves
1 teaspoon black peppercorns
cold water to cover all ingredients

Place bones, onions, carrots and celery in a large roasting pan. Spoon tomato paste over bones and sprinkle with oil. Roast for at least 1 hour in a 220°C oven, or until bones and vegetables are browned. Reduce heat if needed to ensure bones do not burn.

Place roasted mixture, including bones, into a large stock pot with remaining ingredients and cover with cold water approximately 8cm higher than ingredients. Bring to the boil, then reduce to simmer for 2 to 3 hours. Skim occasionally. Strain stock and refrigerate. Remove any solidified fat, then simmer stock uncovered to reduce and intensify flavour if desired. Use within 3 days or freeze.

*chuck, rib or shin bones.

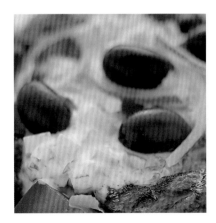

minted yoghurt drizzle

1 cup natural greek style yoghurt
1 clove garlic, crushed
½ continental cucumber, diced
¼ cup fresh mint, finely chopped
cracked black pepper to taste

Combine ingredients and serve.

See recipe page 28.

parsnip mash

400g parsnips, peeled and chopped
2 tablespoons butter
2 medium leeks, halved, washed and
* sliced*
¾ cup cream
cracked black pepper and salt to taste

Place parsnips in a microwaveable bowl. Cover and microwave on high for 5-7 minutes or until parsnips are tender. In a sauté pan, heat butter and add leeks. Cook until soft, then place all ingredients in a food processor and pulse. Serve hot.

See recipe page 29.

roasted capsicums

large capsicums
olive oil to drizzle

Place capsicums in a small roasting pan and drizzle oil on top. Roast in a 200°C oven for 15 to 20 minutes or until capsicum skin has blistered and is starting to blacken.

Put roasted capsicums in a plastic bag and seal. Let stand for at least 10 minutes. This will make the capsicums sweat and release their skin. Peel skin from capsicum and remove stalk and seeds. To store, put capsicums in a clean jar and cover with olive oil or use immediately.

See recipe pages 13 and 27.

capsicum pesto

2 roasted red capsicums, chopped
3 tablespoons olive oil
½ cup fresh mint, roughly chopped
1 clove garlic, chopped
cracked black pepper and salt to taste

Place all ingredients in a blender or food processor and pulse. Do not over process so that capsicum and mint are still chunky.

See recipe page 27.

apple and seeded mustard stuffing

1 tablespoon olive oil
1 medium onion, chopped
1 large red apple, cored and chopped
½ cup dry white wine
1 clove garlic, crushed
100g baguette, thinly sliced and toasted
½ cup vegetable or chicken stock
1 egg, lightly beaten
¼ cup fresh curly parsley, chopped
2 tablespoons seeded mustard

Heat oil in sauté pan and add onion and apple. Sauté until onion is translucent, then add white wine, reduce and remove to cool. Rub raw garlic clove over toasted slices of baguette. Into a bowl add crumbed baguette, apple mixture and remaining ingredients, mix well.

Also great with pork or chicken.

See recipe page 24.

vegetable stock

2 tablespoons olive oil
3 onions, quartered
2 carrots, roughly chopped*
2 leeks, washed and roughly chopped
2 stalks celery, roughly chopped
2 large tomatoes, roughly chopped
8-10 mushrooms (button or other)
3 cloves garlic, bruised
3 sprigs thyme
2 large bay leaves
5 stems fresh parsley (curly or flat)
1 teaspoon black peppercorns
cold water to cover

Heat oil in a large stock pot and add all ingredients except parsley and peppercorns. Sauté vegetables until golden. Add parsley and peppercorns. Cover with cold water ensuring there is enough water to cover ingredients by at least 8cm. Bring to a boil, then reduce to a simmer for 2 to 3 hours. Skim occasionally. Strain stock, discard vegetables and refrigerate. Simmer stock uncovered to reduce and intensify flavour if desired. Use within 3 days or freeze.

You may add any of your favourite root vegetables to suit your taste.

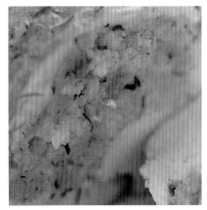

vegetable pickles

½ cup carrot, peeled and grated
1 cup cabbage, finely shredded
½ cup cucumber, julienne
½ cup radish, julienne
½ cup bean sprouts
1 teaspoon fresh ginger, grated
1 tablespoon salt

2 tablespoons white sugar
¼ cup white vinegar

Mix all vegetables and salt together in a bowl, place a weighted plate on top of vegetables and set aside for 1 hour. Rinse salt from vegetables and drain. Add remaining ingredients, mixing well.

See recipe page 45.

cornbread

1½ cups polenta
2 cups plain flour
¼ cup white sugar
2 tablespoons baking powder
1 teaspoon salt
4 large eggs
2 cups buttermilk

Combine dry ingredients. In a separate bowl, lightly beat the eggs with the buttermilk, then add the dry ingredients. Stir mixture only enough to moisten dry ingredients.

Pour mixture into 2 lightly greased 9 inch square or round cake tins. Bake in a 180°C oven for 30 minutes or until golden.

For stuffing
*Halve this recipe for chicken with
    cornbread stuffing, see recipe page 38*

For jalepeno cornbread
¼ cup spring onions, chopped
2 fresh jalepeno chillies, seeded and
    chopped finely **OR**
3 tablespoons bottled jalepeno chillies,
    chopped finely
2 teaspoons cracked black pepper

Add spring onions and jalepenos to buttermilk mixture, then continue with main recipe.

See recipe page 10.

old fashioned turkey gravy

*pan juices from cooked turkey or
    2 tablespoons butter*
2 tablespoons plain flour
2 cups chicken stock
½ cup cream
cracked black pepper and salt to taste

Stir flour into the turkey juices in the roasting pan and gradually add the stock and cream, stirring continuously until sauce has thickened. Add salt and pepper to taste.

If pan juices are not available, melt butter in large sauté pan, add flour and stir continuously for 2 to 3 minutes on low heat. Slowly add stock and cream, stirring until gravy has thickened and is smooth. Add salt and pepper to taste.

See recipe page 48.

orange vinaigrette

½ cup olive oil
juice of 3 oranges
juice of ½ lemon
1 clove garlic, crushed
1 teaspoon coriander seeds,
   finely crushed
pinch of chilli flakes
cracked black pepper and salt to taste

Combine ingredients and whisk.

See recipe page 49.

raspberry chilli jam

1 cup raspberry jam
1 tablespoon chilli paste
1 tablespoon water

Combine ingredients in a microwaveable bowl. Heat in microwave just to warm through – time will depend on individual microwaves, but usually 30 seconds will be sufficient. Serve warm.

See recipe page 42.

chicken stock

2 raw chicken carcasses, chopped
   roughly
1 onion, quartered
2 carrots, roughly chopped
2 stalks celery, roughly chopped
2 sprigs of thyme
2 large bay leaves
4 parsley stems (curly or flat)
peel of ½ lemon (pith removed)
pinch of salt
cold water to cover

Place ingredients in a large stockpot. Cover with cold water to cover ingredients by at least 8cm. Bring to a boil, then reduce to a simmer for 2 hours, covering pot with lid ajar. Skim occasionally. Strain stock and refrigerate. Remove any solidified fat, then simmer stock uncovered to reduce and intensify flavour. Season as desired. Use within 3 days or freeze.

  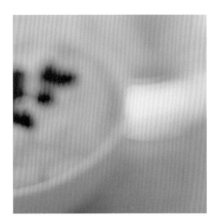

vietnamese dipping sauce

¼ cup fish sauce
2 tablespoons mirin (rice wine vinegar)
2 tablespoons white sugar
1 cup water
1 clove garlic, bruised
½ teaspoon sesame oil
1 small chilli, finely diced
juice of ½ lime
few drops of chilli oil to taste

Combine ingredients and serve with vietnamese pork balls, see page 59.

tarragon vinegar

2 cups white wine vinegar
2 sprigs tarragon

Gently heat the vinegar without bringing to the boil, pour over the tarragon. Store vinegar with tarragon sprigs in an airtight container. Use to drizzle over ham hock soup, see page 57, or use on salads mixed with olive oil.

homemade mayonnaise

1 tablespoon lemon juice
1 egg yolk
1 teaspoon dijon mustard
1 cup vegetable oil
salt and freshly cracked black pepper

In a blender or food processor, combine the lemon juice, egg and mustard, gradually adding oil in a fine stream whilst blender is running. Add salt and pepper to taste.

For rosemary and lemon mayonnaise
    (lamb tarts) – see page 32
Stir 1 teaspoon finely chopped rosemary and grated rind of 1 lemon through mayonnaise.

For capsicum mayonnaise
    (cajun pork) – see page 61
Stir ½ cup diced roasted capsicum and 1 table-spoon chopped fresh oregano through mayonnaise.

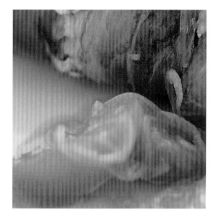

herbed wild and basmati rice

1½ cups basmati and wild rice mix
3 cups chicken or vegetable stock
½ cup fresh mint, chopped
½ cup fresh curly parsley, chopped
½ cup fresh chives, chopped

In a saucepan combine rice and stock. Bring to the boil, then reduce to a low simmer and cover for 15-20 minutes until rice is tender and liquid has absorbed. Remove from heat and add herbs. Serve immediately.

See recipe page 61.

apricot nectar sauce

1 tablespoon butter
1 clove garlic, crushed
½ medium onion, sliced
2 fresh apricots, cut into small wedges*
⅓ cup apricot nectar
2 tablespoons raspberry vinegar
⅓ cup apricot jam

Melt butter on low heat in a sauté pan and add garlic and onion. Cook until onion is translucent, add remaining ingredients. Simmer over low heat for a few minutes to heat apricots through. Serve warm.

*If fresh apricots are unavailable, use 4 tinned halves.

See recipe page 54.

pear and apple relish

1 tablespoon butter
1 clove garlic, crushed
½ medium onion, sliced
1 bay leaf
2 green apples, peeled, cored and diced
2 pears, peeled, cored and diced
2 tablespoons apple cider vinegar
2 tablespoons apple juice
1 tablespoon seeded mustard

Heat butter in a sauté pan and add the garlic, onions and bay leaf. When onion is translucent, add apple and pear. Sauté further for 2 to 3 minutes or until the fruit is slightly browned. Add vinegar and apple juice, then stir in mustard. Remove bay leaf, serve warm or cold.

See recipe page 60.

"everything you wanted to know about meat, but were afraid to ask."

how can you tell if your steak will be tender? What's the best cut of lamb for making kebabs? What is a squab? Where can you buy a boneless chicken? In this section I'll help you to buy, store, prepare and cook your favourite cuts. Read on – it's all here.

hints

general hints for all meats

storing meat and poultry

Meats need to be stored properly, both to retain their nutritional value and to keep them safe. Store all prepackaged foods as directed on the label, and follow these simple rules:

- Use within 2 to 3 days from purchase, or check the use-by-date if applicable
- Store meat and poultry at +5°C or lower
- Freeze meat and poultry you don't intend to use immediately
- I recommend you trim off any excess fat prior to freezing
- Make sure meat and poultry are properly packaged in freezer bags to avoid freezer burn
- For ease of use, divide meat into meal size servings before freezing.

PRODUCT	Approximate Freezer Storage Life (-18°C)
Roasts	4-6 months
Mince	2-3 months
Sausages	1-2 months
Steaks/breasts	2-3 months
Casseroles	2-3 months
Single serve value added products	2-3 months

Although frozen food is safe to eat beyond these times, there may be some loss in eating quality.

thawing and cooking

- Thaw meat and poultry inside the fridge in the crisper or meat drawer, and only defrost in the microwave if using immediately
- Once thawed, cook immediately
- Thawed meat and poultry should never be refrozen in their uncooked state
- If meat is properly cooked in a meal such as a casserole, it is safe to refreeze
- To calculate cooking time for frozen meat, allow approximately 1 hour at 180°C per 500g of meat.

handling and preparation

Bacteria can be passed to and from people, surfaces, food and animals, and even to and from raw and cooked foods. This is known as cross contamination, and can be avoided by following these simple rules:

- Wash hands in hot soapy water for around 30 seconds before preparing foods and after touching raw meat or chicken
- When preparing fresh foods (like salad) and those which are to be cooked (like meat), use a different chopping board and utensils for each. If you have only one chopping board, wash it well with soapy water and rinse in chilled water before re-using
- Use different utensils for cooked foods
- Never place cooked foods in unwashed receptacles which have previously contained raw products such as meat, poultry or fish.

cooking

- Most people will eat 200-250g of meat in a single meal

- Most larger cuts of meat and roasts will take approximately one hour per kilogram to cook in an oven at 180°C. Rare beef will take approximately 45 minutes per kilogram

- Some cooks believe that sealing meat at a higher temperature first helps maintain flavour and moisture. It certainly doesn't do any harm

- When cooking mince, sausages, hamburgers and rolled roasts ensure that they are cooked right through and there is no pink inside. If unsure, use a meat thermometer to check the internal temperature – it should be around 75°C when properly cooked

- The secret of a really successful casserole or stew is to cook it slowly at a lower temperature, around 2 to 3 hours at 150°C

- When cooking larger portions of meat like a roast, allow it to settle for 5-10 minutes before carving – it makes a big difference

- When cooking corned meat, it is often wise to rinse first in chilled water to remove excess salt

- Enclosing joints and roasts in an oven bag during cooking will help maintain moisture and assist in keeping your oven clean.

Compiled with assistance from Meat and Livestock Australia, Australian Chicken Meat Federation Inc. and Australian Pork Corporation.

buying beef

When talking about beef, probably the most asked question is "how do I tell what is a good cut of meat and whether it will be tender or not?"

There is no easy answer without going into enormous detail, but these days Meat and Livestock Australia (MLA) and the cattle industry have removed a lot of the guesswork through the introduction of Meat Standards Australia (MSA). This joint initiative is a grading system that ensures consumers can buy beef with the confidence that what they have purchased will meet their expectations. By tracking all the processes in beef production from paddock to plate, they have been able to isolate the factors that ensure good eating.

MSA accredited butchers sell quality meat that guarantees tenderness or your money back. Most progressive butcher shops are already operating under this scheme and, I expect in time, all meat stores will supply officially sanctioned beef. It is well worth looking around your local area to find an MSA accredited butcher, because, as well as guaranteeing tenderness, they will also give you advice about the best methods for cooking the particular cut you have purchased. Ring the MSA consumer hotline on 1800 550 019 to find the closest accredited butcher to you.

As life moves at a much greater pace these days, our needs and expectations are continually changing. Kitchen knowledge is slowly being lost and the onus for quality is moving back to the establishments from whom we purchase our food. The introduction of MSA makes our calculated decision regarding the purchase of beef that much easier.

cut by cut

We all know rib fillet, rump, sirloin and eye fillet – they are on the menu of every restaurant we go into. However, there is a lot more to beef than steak, so here are some of the more common cuts, the best ways of cooking them, what to look for when purchasing and what part of the animal they come from.

tenderloin (eye fillet)

Origin:

Inside of the hind quarter.

Visual:

Pink/red colouring with some marbling (fine seams of fat). The meat should be firm. If it doesn't hold its shape well or is a dark red to purple, it means that the cut has most likely come off older beef.

Cooking:

The eye fillet is the most tender of the beef cuts and melts in your mouth, but it doesn't have a lot of natural flavour. Therefore, it is best grilled or pounded out for pan frying with a sauce. You can roast it, but if you do, cut it thickly or roast it whole.

striploin (sirloin, porterhouse, new york cut)

Origin:

The striploin is an outside cut that runs down the backbone along the vertebrae.

Visual:

The flesh of the striploin should be an opaque, pink colour. A high level of marbling and a good even layer of fat will enhance flavour.

Cooking:

Striploin is ideal for roasting, grilling and for stir-fry. Unlike most beef, It will tend to toughen if cooked slowly over time, so I don't advise using it for casseroles or stews. It is a premium cut and generally regarded as second only to the tenderloin.

scotch fillet/cube roll

Origin:

The scotch fillet is an outside cut from the fore quarter that runs down the backbone.

Visual:

As with the tenderloin (eye fillet), the meat should be firm with fine marbling and an even layer of white flaky fat. If the fat's yellow, the meat has come from an older animal.

Cooking:

Scotch fillet has more flavour than the tenderloin and is great eaten 'au naturelle' or with a sauce or dressing. It also grills and roasts well and is suitable for stir-fry if sliced thinly.

rump

Origin:

If you can't guess this one we have a problem!

Visual:

Good, flavoursome, rump usually is enhanced by strong marbling. It should have a fine, even layer of white fat covering the top and firm pinkish flesh. Aged rump will be a bit darker in colour.

Cooking:

Great for grilling, however it roasts just as well. The whole rump can be divided into four or five other muscles. The rump cap is good for roasting and if you don't believe me, try the feature recipe with thai curry and coconut in the beef section. The eye of the rump and the centre muscle are good roasting but also great for grilling, while the triangular tip of the rump, interestingly enough called the tritip, is a really good grilling piece.

t-bone

Origin:

The T-Bone is made up of the striploin and tenderloin left on the bone and cut crossways.

Visual:

The meat should be firmly attached to the bone, which should be white with some pink speckling. The meat will be a little bit darker red in colour.

Cooking:

An old favourite, and one of the best steaks for grilling.

topside

Origin:

Another hind-quarter cut, just above the backend of the animal

Visual:

Topside will be a darker red in colour and should have a good fat covering.

Cooking:

Makes great mince, and can be used for stir-fry or for roasting at a low temperature for a long time. Like the eye round, it has a coarse grained texture and can tend to break up into stringy pieces when cooked. Check out the couple of Asian recipes using topside, the beef broth and the marinated beef.

knuckle
(round whole)

Origin:

As the name suggests this cut comes from near a joint, in this case the inside of the back leg.

Visual:

Shaped a bit like a football (Aussie Rules of course!). It should be very lean and a light to medium pink in colour.

Cooking:

The knuckle makes a fabulous little roast, and is also ideal for stir-fry and casseroles. If you can find a small knuckle, cut crossways, it will even make a good steak for the barbecue (round steak).

blade

Origin:

Part of the forequarter, the blade lays along the outside of the shoulder.

Visual:

A rectangular cut that is pink/red in colour and pale on the surface.

Cooking:

Blade has lots of flavour and is great for roasts and stews if cooked slowly on a lower temperature (150°C). Like topside, it is terrific for lean beef mince. It is a paler colour than most cuts when cooked.

oyster blade

Origin:

A cut from the blade containing the flinch muscle.

Visual:

Oyster blade is a little bit darker with some marbling. Very lean, the grain of the blade runs lengthways, so it is essential to cut it across the grain.

Cooking:

Again, lots of flavour. If you can be bothered removing the connective tissue and cut it into strips, it will stir-fry well. Oyster blade will grill quite nicely or can roast well if left whole.

chuck

Origin:

Chuck comes from the neck end of the animal.

Visual:

It has a slightly darker flesh and is cylindrical in shape.

Cooking:

Great for mince as it is full of flavour. It doesn't break down easily, so it needs to be cooked slowly for 2 to 3 hours. Great for curries and casseroles.

chuck tender

Origin:

Chuck tender comes from the blade.

Visual:

Conical in shape, again with slightly darker flesh.

Cooking:

Like the chuck, this is best slow cooked and great for pot roasts, curries and stews.

brisket

Origin:

The brisket comes from the fore quarter and can best be described as the breast plate of the animal, stretching back to the flank region.

Visual:

A flat rectangular piece of meat about 3cms deep, with a layer of meat, a layer of fat and lots of tissue.

Cooking:

The brisket has lots of flavour, and is excellent for braising or for making beef stock. It is also excellent marinated, rolled or corned. Try the recipe in the beef section – it is one of my favourites.

silverside

Origin:

Silverside is found below the rump.

Visual:

Made up of the eye round and the outside, the eye will be lighter in colour and the outside darker. Silverside will usually have a fine cap of fat.

Cooking:

This is a coarse grained cut of meat, but because of its moistness will roast or slow cook quite well. The silverside is probably best known as the most common cut for corned beef.

eye round (girello)

Origin:

Eye round comes from the butt of the animal, much the same area as the rump.

Visual:

This is a very lean cut, pink/red in colour, with a small amount of connective tissue on the outside.

Cooking:

Eye round roasts quite well as a whole piece or makes great corned beef. Cut into strips, it can make a good stir-fry, or diced, it also works well in a casserole or for braising. I wouldn't pan fry this product as it has a stringy texture and will tend to dry out unless sauced or cooked with added moisture.

cheek

Origin:

As the name suggests, it can only come from one of two places and it isn't the nether region.

Visual:

The cheek is a darkish, oval shaped cut with a very coarse texture and a tight grain.

Cooking:

This is one of the most flavoursome cuts for slow braising, and has recently become trendy in many well known restaurants.

nutrition

Today's beef cuts are packed full of nutrients. Trimmed of visible fat, they are generally lean with low cholesterol levels. Only about half of us eat beef at the recommended frequency. It is recommended that we eat lean red meat 3-4 times a week to maintain good levels of protein and nutrients. Lean beef can certainly have a place in the diet of people with heart disease or at risk of heart disease.

Protein

Red meat is our most important source of protein.

Vitamin B

Vitamin B helps our nervous system function and helps in the production of DNA which carries our genetic code.

Iron

Red meat is a great source of iron, particularly haem iron which is easily absorbed by our bodies and not found in vegetables. Iron helps blood cells carry oxygen to our muscles and also helps turn glucose into energy. These processes aid brain development and function.

Zinc

Zinc is an antioxidant and important for bone and hair formation, wound healing, and helping our immune system ward off infections.

Omega – 3 Fatty Acids

Good for brain and heart function

quality assurance- is the beef we're eating safe?

Australia is the largest exporter of cattle in the world and has embraced comprehensive quality assurance programs to ensure protection of our domestic and export industry. Australian livestock producers are also among the world's leaders in advanced animal husbandry and production techniques.

Strict quarantine regulations have ensured that Australian cattle remain contaminant free. To support the various government regulations that ensure our livestock remains of the highest quality, the local cattle industry has also developed its own quality assurance program called Cattlecare. This is a strict code of practice based on the principles of HACCP. Underpinning all this is Australia's comprehensive identification system, used to trace the origin of all purpose grown livestock.

Compiled with assistance from Meat and Livestock Australia.

lamb

buying lamb

Meat and Livestock Australia (MLA) and the Sheepmeat Council of Australia (SCA) are currently working on defining and improving lamb eating quality. Whether this will ultimately end up in a program like Meat Standards Australia has achieved for beef remains to be seen. The quality of lamb doesn't perhaps have the same variables as beef and may be controllable at industry level, but I think a similar program would definitely help consumers with their lamb selection.

There are some very basic things to look for when buying lamb. Lamb meat has a clear pinkish bloom (sheen) that deepens as the animal grows older. Reddish purple flesh usually determines mutton and should the "lamb" meat have lost its lustre and be turning brown, forget it. "Truth in labelling" these days means that lamb and mutton will generally be as ticketed in the shop. Any fat should be firmly attached to the meat and be white rather than cream in colour.

A general guide for determining true lamb is that it will be branded with a red dye. No branding means the product is mutton. This is just a guide, however, as sometimes unbranded export lamb appears in the domestic market place.

cut by cut

lamb leg

Origin:

The leg is fairly obvious. These days it may be separated into several different primals as well (topside, rump, knuckle and silverside)

Cooking:

As the more conventional whole leg, bone in or boneless and rolled, roasting is by far the best option. The knuckle, topside and rump also make beautiful little roasts, and can be sliced for stir-fry or diced for kebabs.

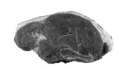

chump

Origin:

The chump is the flesh section at the top of the leg near the hipbone.

Cooking:

As a trimmed whole muscle (rump), the chump is good for roasting. Sweet tasting chump chops are great on the barbecue, pan-fried, grilled or casseroled. Try the Moroccan lamb if you enjoy a little spice.

loin

Origin:

Outside cut that runs down the backbone along the vertebrae. Both loins together on the bone are known as the saddle. The eye of the loin is known as the eye muscle or back strap and is the tenderest part of lamb. Loin chops have little meat but are extremely sweet in flavour.

Cooking:

Whole loin makes a great seasoned roast. Butterflied steaks from the backstrap can be barbecued or pan fried. Cutlets (also known as French cutlets) are cut from the loin and are excellent for crumbing individually or for roasting whole as a rack of lamb. Loin chops have very little meat but are extremely sweet in flavour.

forequarter

Origin:

The forequarter is derived from the front part of the lamb back to the fifth rib. This incorporates the shoulder, eye muscle, neck and shank.

Cooking:

Boned and rolled forequarter with fat removed makes a very sweet roast. Forequarter chops (BBQ chops) have quite a lot of bone and sinew but great flavour, ideal if you enjoy picking up the bone and taking your time.

The shank has become trendy in restaurants and is best when sauced and slow cooked or braised. Ask your butcher to French them (clean the bone and trim the fat) for better presentation.

shoulder

Origin:

The shoulder includes the shoulder blade and front shank of the animal.

Cooking:

Boneless and rolled shoulder is good for roasting. Alternatively, minced shoulder is great for hamburgers and sausages.

shank

Origin:

The lower fore and hind legs.

Cooking:

The shank is great in soups or braised with a sauce. Try the chunky tomato soup with lamb shanks in the lamb section and you'll know what I mean.

best neck chops

Origin:

Best neck chops come from the lower neck area comprising the first 3-4 ribs.

Cooking:

Neck chops are bony and marbled with fat but have very good flavour. They are best cooked on low temperature for a long time, such as in soups and casseroles. Also nice crumbed.

rack

Origin:

The rack comes from the rib area of the lamb, and should consist of 6-9 ribs. Ask your butcher to French the rack – this will remove excess fat and individualise each rib for easy cutting when cooked.

Cooking:

Rack of lamb is best for roasting but is also great cooked on any enclosed barbecue.

specialty cuts

Where from:

Let's not go into details! Lambs brains, liver, kidneys and so on are considered delicacies by many and are finding their way back onto some of the most exclusive menus in the country.

Cooking:

Most commonly pan-fried, specialty cuts may also be sauced, seasoned or stuffed. If you've never tried lambs fry, I guarantee the recipe with roasted capsicum pesto will win you for life.

nutrition

Today's trim lamb cuts are packed full of nutrients and not high in fat, being generally lean with low cholesterol levels. It is recommended that we eat lean red meat 3-4 times a week to maintain good levels of protein and nutrients. Trim lamb has a place in the diet of people with heart disease or at risk of heart disease.

Protein

Red meat is our most important source of protein.

Vitamin B

Vitamin B helps our nervous system function and helps in the production of DNA which carries our genetic code.

Iron

Red meat is a great source of iron, particularly haem iron which is easily absorbed by our bodies and not found in vegetables. Iron helps blood cells carry oxygen to our muscles and also helps turn glucose into energy. These processes aid brain development and function.

Zinc

Zinc is an antioxidant and important for bone and hair formation, wound healing, and helping our immune system ward off infections.

Omega – 3 Fatty Acids

Good for brain and heart function

quality assurance for lamb

To guarantee the delivery of a quality, consistent product, it is vital that all aspects of production, processing and delivery of food, are of assured standards. The sheep industry monitors and audits through the Flockcare system.

This is a relatively new program designed to help lamb producers meet agreed standards, and takes into account food safety, chemicals and residues, animal health, husbandry and welfare, presentation and animal transport. Flockcare members are subject to independent or third party audits that guarantee the integrity of their product.

These days we can be comfortable in the knowledge that lamb producers are ensuring the lamb we eat is only of the highest quality.

Compiled with assistance from Meat and Livestock Australia.

fowl

buying poultry

The poultry industry has been a lot easier to regulate than beef and lamb because of the animal's size. Feed intake can be controlled and strict breeding practices mean we end up with a very consistent product.

Poultry should always look smooth, with the breast being pliable and having an opaque pale pink bloom. Avoid grey looking breasts of chicken or chicken that's sticky to the touch. The thigh should be rich pink in colour.

Although supermarket poultry is usually consistent, it doesn't compare with the fresh product purchased from a specialist like Lenard's. Don't be fooled into buying poultry on the bone as a cheaper alternative – with the bone removed, the chicken meat will usually be a similar price to the filleted product.

whole chicken

Sizing:

Size determines the weight of chicken. A size 12 chicken weighs 1.2kg, a size 16 weighs 1.6kg and so on.

Cooking:

Whole chicken may be roasted, kettle barbecued or boiled. Even today it is hard to go past a seasoned roast chicken.

breast and tenderloin

Origin:

The breast is the fleshy meat on the upper side of the carcass. The tenderloin is the strip of meat attached to the underside of the breast.

Visual:

Opaque pink to white flesh, a good sheen, not sticky to touch and well trimmed of fat.

Cooking:

The breast may be roasted, stir-fried, pan fried or casseroled. Extremely versatile whether on or off the bone, it can dry out if overcooked. Some people cook breast with the skin attached to assist maintaining moisture in the product. Try the teriyaki chicken with sesame biscuits, you won't be disappointed.

thigh

Origin:

The thigh is the fleshy meat on the upper part of the leg.

Visual:

Deep raspberry pink colour, not sticky to touch and well trimmed of fat.

Cooking:

The thigh fillet may be crumbed for schnitzel, stir-fried, pan fried or casseroled. It is also ideal for making kebabs. The thigh is more succulent than the breast and has more flavour. Whereas the breast tends to turn white when cooked, the thigh will usually lighten but it is not uncommon for the thigh to hold its colour when cooked.

maryland

Origin:

The maryland is the cut comprising the drumstick and thigh conjoined.

Visual:

Visible flesh should be deep pink. Skin should be white rather than grey.

Cooking:

The maryland is best roasted, pan fried or braised. More flavoursome than the breast, it can tend to dry out if overcooked. Try the recipe with dates and prosciutto.

drumstick

Origin:

The drumstick is the fleshy lower leg of the chicken.

Visual:

Visible flesh should be deep pink. Skin should be white rather than grey.

Cooking:

The drumstick is best marinated and roasted, pan fried or casseroled. As with the thigh, the drumstick is a more succulent meat than the breast.

thigh cutlet

Origin:

The thigh cutlet is the whole thigh with all bone bar the central leg bone removed.

Visual:

Visible flesh should be deep pink. Skin should be white rather than grey.

Cooking:

The cutlet may be roasted, stir-fried, pan fried or casseroled. Some people cook the cutlet with the skin attached to assist in maintaining moisture.

wing

Origin:

The wing is attached to the fleshy upper end of the chicken.

Visual:

Skin should be white rather than grey, not sticky to touch and have pink red tips, not brown.

Cooking:

The wing may be marinated and roasted, pan fried or casseroled.

turkey

Sizing:

A 20 range turkey is between 2-3kg, 30 range between 3-4kg and so on.

Visual:

Opaque grey/pink colour to the skin.

Cooking:

Turkey is best oven baked or kettle barbecued. It is a good idea to cover the legs and wings with foil on larger birds to avoid burning.

duck and other game birds

QUAIL or POUSSIN are very small game birds that are best cooked whole or split in half.

SPATCHCOCK is young chicken.

PIGEON is also known as squab.

GOOSE and DUCK, as with a lot of wild birds, can tend to be somewhat fatty and are usually best cooked in a way which allows excess fat to disperse, such as boiled, roasted on a spit or on a rack in the oven. The Asian glazed duck in the fowl section is sensational.

nutrition

For the purpose of this nutritional analysis we have used chicken as the most common fowl variety. Chicken is extremely dense in nutrients, including protein, zinc, iron, phosphorous, riboflavin, thiamin and niacin.

Energy:

100g of baked chicken will give around 9% of the recommended dietary intake for energy.

Protein:

An excellent source of protein, a 100g serve will supply around half the recommended dietary intake.

Fat

Fat in chicken is greatly reduced by removing the skin. Skinless breast fillet with fat removed can be lower than 1% fat content.

Cholesterol

Breast has lowest cholesterol at around 62mg/100g.

Minerals:

Chicken contains significant quantities of many minerals, including iron, zinc, magnesium and phosphorous.

quality assurance

Improved processing methods over the past two decades have ensured that chicken is as safe as any other form of meat. As most chicken meat is grown, bred and prepared for sale at the same manufacturer, it is easier to control the processes for poultry production. None the less, major producers like Bartter Steggles have very stringent HACCP based quality assurance programs in place.

hormones and antibiotics

While I'm on the subject of quality assurance, I would also like to dispel a couple of myths about chicken in Australia.

Hormones.

Hormones were banned from chicken production in Australia back in the early 1960's and have not been used since.

There has long been a misconception regarding hormones in chicken meat, probably stimulated by some overseas documentaries on the subject. While being unable to comment on practices overseas, the Australian Chicken Meat Federation has categorically advised that all chickens used for chicken meat in Australia are hormone free.

A Commonwealth Government testing program regularly checks for hormone residues in feed. Interestingly, many years ago, when oestrogen was administered for a time, it was for the purpose of neutering male birds and not as a growth promotant as many people believe. Today the practice of administering oestrogen to produce capons is banned universally.

Advertising of poultry as "hormone free" has also probably fuelled the misconception as all poultry in Australia is free from hormones and has been for nearly four decades.

Antibiotics.

Use of antibiotics has been diminishing since the early 1970's. Antibiotics are only used if a severe bacterial infection occurs, with vaccines being used as a deterrent and generally regarded as a much more user friendly alternative. Even when antibiotics are necessary, only those approved by the National Health and Medical Research Council and the National Registration Authority are used, with all residue levels being strictly monitored.

Thirdly, chickens used in chicken meat production in Australia are farmed in warehouse size sheds and basically have the run of the place. For the animal's wellbeing, it has been found that it is preferable for the birds to be housed and protected from the elements. Government policy for animal welfare ensures that chicken meat production, particularly by the major producers, is controlled by strict regulation.

Compiled with assistance from
Chicken Meat Federation Australia Inc and Bartter Steggles.

buying pork

Pork can be a much maligned meat and really doesn't deserve the reputation. Controlled farming of pigs in Australia ensures that the quality and safety of pork is of the highest standard.

Pork meat should be pale pink to deep pink in colour depending upon the size of the pig or what part of the animal it comes from. When shopping for pork, ask for retail pork rather than bacon pork which comes from larger pigs. The smaller the pig, the more succulent and flavoursome the meat. Asian butchers, in particular, tend only to deal with smaller pork.

There is nothing better than a good old fashioned pork chop with lashings of apple sauce, but the leaner, boneless, skinless, "New-Fashioned Pork" is much more versatile.

leg

Origin:

Self explanatory. This can be a very large joint and is often cut in half, the fleshier fillet end and the hock end. Alternatively it can be broken down into the muscle cuts, outside, inside, knuckle and rump.

Visual:

Small retail pork legs. Flesh should be light pink and dry. Fat should be white and the skin a pale pink colour.

Cooking:

The pork leg cuts, make great roasts. Ask your butcher to score the skin deeply for crackling, and rub with oil and salt before cooking to make it crisp. Diced leg is good for casseroles or cut into strips or fine slices makes great stir-fry. Leg portions, flattened out and crumbed, also make great pork schnitzel.

boneless pork loin

Origin:

Outside cut that runs down the back-bone along the vertebrae.

Visual:

Pale pink flesh, not too large a layer of white fat under the skin.

Cooking:

Rolled and stuffed makes a great roast, either with skin on or off. I especially like the nectarine stuffing with the recipe at the back of the pork section. Loin chops are best grilled or pan fried.

fillet (tenderloin)

Origin:

Muscles from the belly surface of the lumbar vertebrae. Very tender cut.

Visual:

Pale pink meat in a long strip.

Cooking:

May be cooked as a whole portion or cut into pieces. Like chicken breast, it cooks very quickly. May be oven cooked with sauce, great in stir-fry of for kebabs. Can also be flattened into steaks for pan-frying with sauce.

spareribs (pork belly)

Origin:

The spareribs are cut from inside the thick end of the pork belly.

Visual:

Reasonable amount of darker pink meat.

Cooking:

Often heavily spiced, spareribs are best roasted or braised slowly until the meat is just about falling off the bone. Look for the spare ribs with bourbon and maple as you are going through the recipes.

chump

Origin:

The fleshy upper part of the leg.

Visual:

Pale pink flesh, not too large a layer of white fat.

Cooking:

As a whole joint, a beautiful sweet roast either bone-in or boneless. The chump chop is extremely versatile and good for grilling, pan-frying, casseroles and barbecues.

shoulder

Origin:

Self explanatory.

Visual:

Lean deeper pink meat with marbling.

Cooking:

The shoulder is usually split up into chops and a roast called the collar butt. Rolled and tied makes a nice full flavoured, sweet roast.

nutrition

- New fashioned pork, trimmed of fat and skin, is full of essential nutrients.
- Pork contains necessary levels of iron, thiamine, riboflavin and is high in protein.
- Improved production techniques in recent years has seen the overall fat content of pork reduced by around 65%.
- Any lean cut of pork contains less 0.1% cholesterol making it a great meat for all types of diets.

quality assurance

Australian breeding techniques for pork are judged to be at the leading edge by world standards. Most pigs are housed indoors and fed primarily on quality grains to ensure a consistent healthy animal. The Pig Research and Development Corporation is dedicated completely to improving the efficiency and standards of pork production.

Compiled with assistance from Australian Pork Corporation.

glossary terms

blanch
To cook raw ingredients briefly in boiling water, then plunge into cold water or drain.

bruise
To crush with the flat of a knife to release flavour, eg garlic.

butterflied
To split a food down the middle almost completely through, and flatten it out to resemble a butterfly.

deglaze
To add a small amount of wine or stock to a pan in which meat has been cooked in order to make a base for gravy or a sauce.

grain of meat
The direction of the fibres.

infuse
To steep or soak an aromatic item in order to extract its flavour.

julienne
To cut into thin slivers or sticks.

marinade
Seasoned liquid in which meat, fish or vegetables are soaked to enhance flavour or tenderise before cooking.

reduce
To rapidly boil a liquid in order to lessen volume and concentrate flavour.

refresh
To plunge partially cooked vegetables or fruit into cold water to prevent further cooking or help retain colour.

sealing meat
To brown meat quickly in hot oil or butter in order to seal in the juices and to retain good flavour and colour.

sauté
To fry food quickly in a small amount of hot oil or fat.

score
To make shallow cuts on the surface of foods, eg: pork fat for crackling.

truss
To tie meat with kitchen string so that it retains its shape when cooking.

tenderise
Pounding meat with a mallet to soften fibres.

zest
The coloured outer rind of citrus fruits. Used to flavour foods. May be cut into thin strips or julienne.

hints
Garlic may be omitted in any recipe.

Soak wooden skewers in water to prevent burning.

Always preheat oven to required temperature.

glossary

the team

I would like to extend my sincerest thanks to everybody who has given time and effort toward making this book possible.

Special thanks go to:

Project Management   Lynette Rattray

Design and Art Direction   Jack Pavey

Photography   Heather Dinas

Recipe Concepts, Development and all Styling   Theresa Stastny

Assistant to Stylist   Bethany Heald

Recipe Concepts and Development   Lenard's Executive Chef, Brian Pozzey

Editor   Astrid Sweres

Lenard's Creative Writer   Malcolm Hickman

Typesetting   Scarlet Star Projects

Graphic Reproduction   Colorific Lithographics Pty Ltd, Melbourne

Printing   Braemar Colour Printers, Melbourne

Binding   Marvel Bookbinders, Melbourne

Packaging   The Packaging Company, Melbourne

many thanks to all the people who helped us:

Des Young at Peter Bouchier Butchers, Malvern Road, Toorak (MSA accredited),

The Willows Restaurant, 462 St Kilda Road, Melbourne.

Hospitality Dinnerware, Prahran. Minimax, Toorak. Supply and Demand, Richmond for Props.

To the staff at Lenard's national office who have all contributed in one way or another.

index

... where to from here?

i said back in the beginning, nothing really changes, it just re-invents itself. The beef, lamb, pork and poultry industries are currently going through this process of re-invention. They have expended a lot of energy at the growing and production end of their business but it is now time to shift the emphasis to you, the consumer.

the take away and restaurant markets have benefited from picking the eyes out of the meat industry for the last thirty years and it is time that the meat industry, collectively, looked at processes that will ensure good quality and wholesome meat products are readily available for the home consumer. After all, the majority of meals are still eaten in the home.

i'm pleased to say that there are some very positive signs in this direction. The introduction of Meat Standards Australia for beef has been a great step forward, while improved production techniques for the poultry, lamb and pork industries are creating much more user friendly products. The different factions of the meat industry all understand what has to be done to meet the needs of our changing lifestyles, the challenge lies in how they go about doing it.

i have always been a strong advocate of allowing the consumer to tell me what they want and the message I'm getting is telling me that you want food made even easier in the kitchen, backed up by a good quality product, friendly informative service and a brand you can trust.

wouldn't it be great to drop into your local convenience centre and pick up a fresh osso bucco or a thai green curry already cooked and packaged so all you had to do was heat it in the microwave for 10 minutes, to have a solution to the evening meal? Wouldn't it make life easy if you could have a tandoori chicken or greek lamb in the refrigerator just in case some friends dropped in?

this is where I believe the industry is heading and the good news is that it's just around the corner. This is the way of the future and as usual Lenard's is leading the way. These days we are not only preparing your meat but cooking it as well. I call it Lenard's *easyliving* range and I believe that it answers your need for tasty, wholesome products without the time and the fuss required when preparing a meal from scratch.

so if there are not enough hours in the day to prepare a quality home cooked meal, if you find the kitchen more pressure than pleasure, don't despair. After all, the aromas and memories of great food shared with good friends or family can be only as far away as your local Lenard's store.